LOTS OF THINGS
TO KNOW ABOUT
DINOSAURS

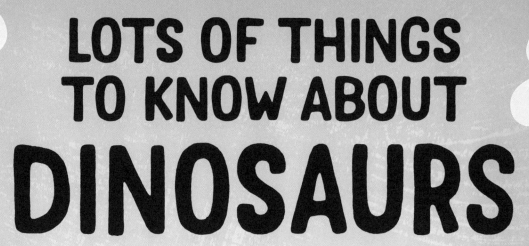

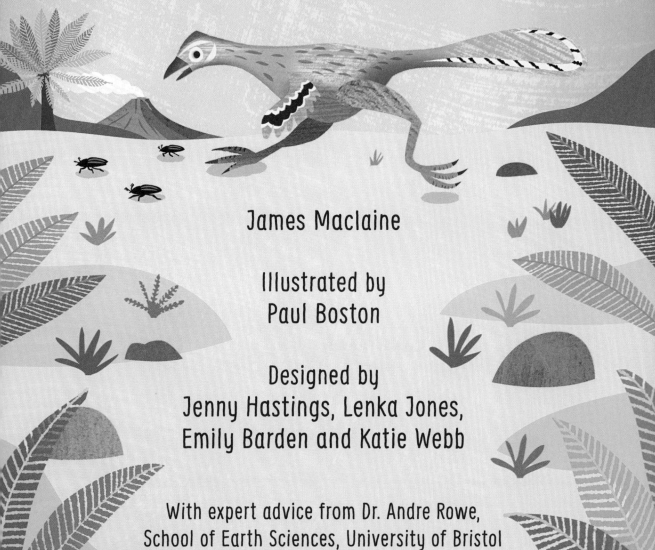

James Maclaine

Illustrated by
Paul Boston

Designed by
Jenny Hastings, Lenka Jones,
Emily Barden and Katie Webb

With expert advice from Dr. Andre Rowe,
School of Earth Sciences, University of Bristol

USBORNE QUICKLINKS

Scan the code for links to websites with
exciting dinosaur videos, activities and facts,
or go to **usborne.com/Quicklinks** and
type in the title of this book.

You can also listen to someone saying the names
of all the dinosaurs in this book at Usborne Quicklinks.

Please follow the internet safety guidelines at Usborne Quicklinks.
Children should be supervised online.

Did you know that scientists keep discovering
fossils of new types of dinosaurs, such as
Changmiania, which was found recently in China?

Long, long, long, long, long, LONG ago

To help you to imagine just how far back you'd need to go to meet **living** dinosaurs, follow this line as it spirals down the page...

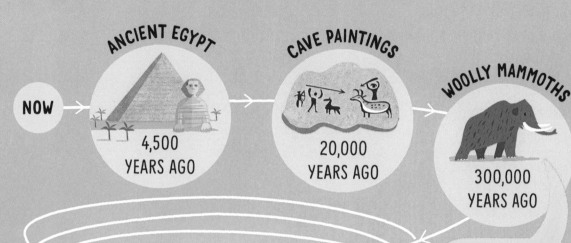

NOW

ANCIENT EGYPT
4,500 YEARS AGO

CAVE PAINTINGS
20,000 YEARS AGO

WOOLLY MAMMOTHS
300,000 YEARS AGO

Dinosaurs? I've never seen one. You still need to go 250 times further back in time.

1 MILLION YEARS AGO

10 MILLION YEARS AGO

30 MILLION YEARS AGO

DINOSAURS
BETWEEN 66 AND 250 MILLION YEARS AGO

Hello. You've reached us at last.

Dinosaur times

Even if you've seen it on television or in a film, Stegosaurus never met Triceratops — and Tyrannosaurus rex never chased Diplodocus! That's because dinosaurs didn't all live at the same time. Some were separated from each other by **millions** and **millions** of years.

You can see the **whole** time that dinosaurs were around on the pages of this unusual calendar...

Dinosaur times are divided into three stages: Triassic, Jurassic and Cretaceous.

Aha!

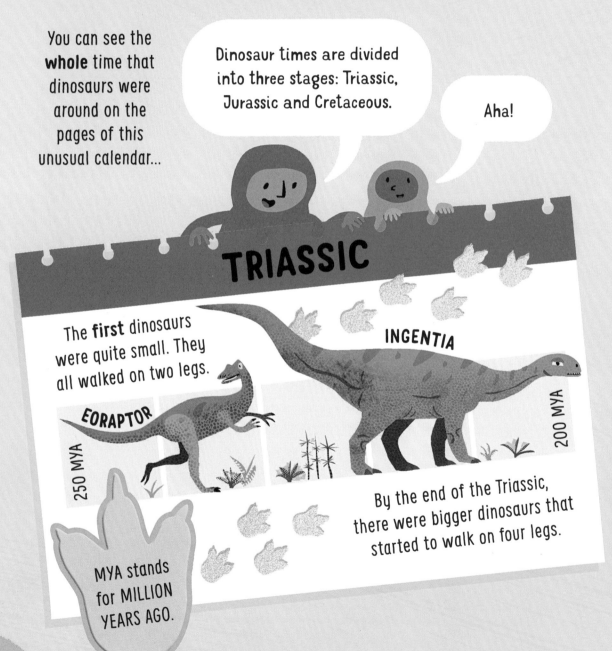

TRIASSIC

The **first** dinosaurs were quite small. They all walked on two legs.

INGENTIA

EORAPTOR

250 MYA

200 MYA

By the end of the Triassic, there were bigger dinosaurs that started to walk on four legs.

MYA stands for MILLION YEARS AGO.

JURASSIC

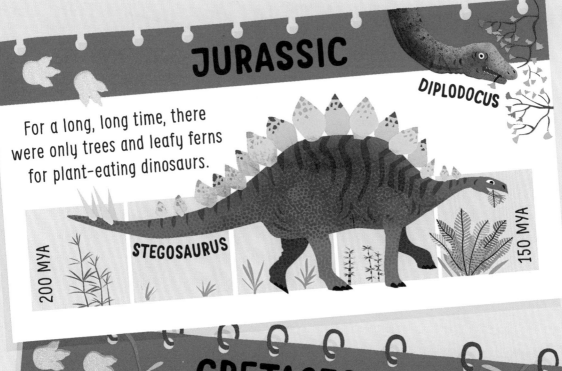

For a long, long time, there were only trees and leafy ferns for plant-eating dinosaurs.

DIPLODOCUS

STEGOSAURUS

200 MYA

150 MYA

CRETACEOUS

IGUANODON

Then, later on, the first flowers bloomed.

150 MYA

100 MYA

TYRANNOSAURUS REX

And when the last dinosaurs arrived there were ants, bees and butterflies, too.

TRICERATOPS

100 MYA

66 MYA

What dinosaurs ACTUALLY looked like

Ancient living things sometimes left behind rock-like remains called **fossils**. The fossils left by dinosaurs don't always show the whole picture, but they give lots of clues. They show...

...the shapes of their bodies

...the lengths of their claws

...how many teeth they had

...and that some dinosaurs were covered in feathers.

But all the **colours** in the dinosaur pictures on this page are total guesses.

No one really knows which dinosaurs were red, yellow, pink, green, purple, brown or blue — except for a very few types. Such as, Psittacosaurus...

Scientists found enough **skin** in a fossil of this dinosaur to work out its colours and patterns.

PSITTACOSAURUS FOSSIL

PSITTACOSAURUS

What are those yellow spikes on its tail?

They were found in the fossil too. They're called bristles.

Dinosaurs the size of rabbits

Did you know that **some** dinosaurs were **small** enough to hold in your arms? To understand just how little they could be, you could compare them with more familiar animals...

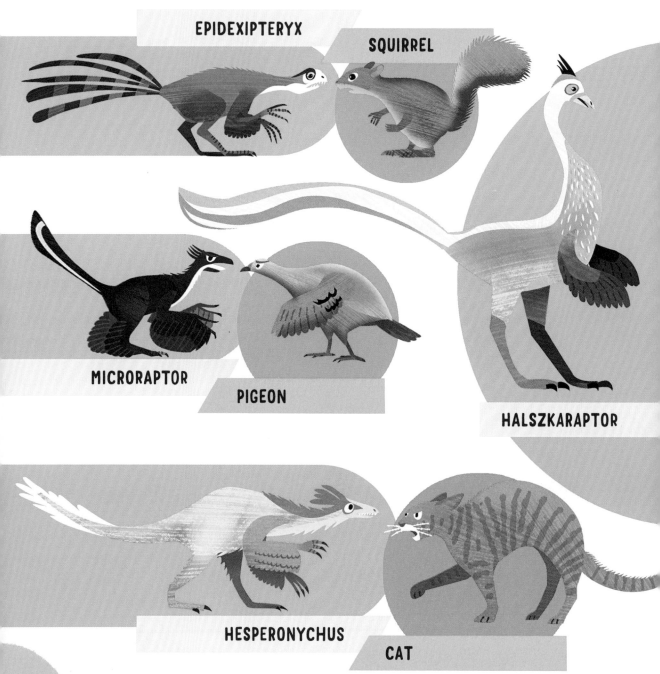

EPIDEXIPTERYX

SQUIRREL

MICRORAPTOR

PIGEON

HALSZKARAPTOR

HESPERONYCHUS

CAT

DUCK

MEI

How much bigger were the BIGGEST dinosaurs?

Hundreds of times longer and thousands of times heavier! We'll meet the giants on pages 16-17.

TURKEY

RABBIT

AQUILOPS

9

What's the point of a dinosaur's tail?

Every single type of dinosaur had a **tail**.

Some tails were very, very, **very** long.

Apatosaurus had a long body and a long neck — but its tail was even longer.

Most of the time, dinosaurs held their tails up in the air. They only left tail tracks on the ground if they crouched down.

DILOPHOSAURUS

One fossil shows marks made in the sand by a Dilophosaurus's tail.

Long tails helped dinosaurs with heavy bodies to keep their balance.

Without my tail, I'd have fallen onto my face!

APATOSAURUS

And this dinosaur wagged its tail from side to side, so it could run **faster**.

COELOPHYSIS

If you don't have a tail, swinging your arms can help you to speed up!

If only I had a tail...

How to tell what dinosaurs ate

You could find out if a dinosaur ate **meat** or **plants** by checking the way it walked.

All the meat-eating dinosaurs walked on **two legs**. They had much smaller arms.

There were plant eaters who used two legs, too, but most of them walked on **four**.

JUICY MEAT

LUSH PLANTS

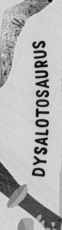

DYSALOTOSAURUS

Please come back! I only eat leaves – I promise.

So, four legs safe, two legs... and it might be time to...

RUN!!

Inside a dinosaur's tummy

If you could go on a journey through a Caudipteryx's body, you'd be surprised when you reached its tummy...

Dinosaurs in shining armour

So that they didn't end up a meat eater's next meal, these dinosaurs had tough body parts that worked like a suit of armour.

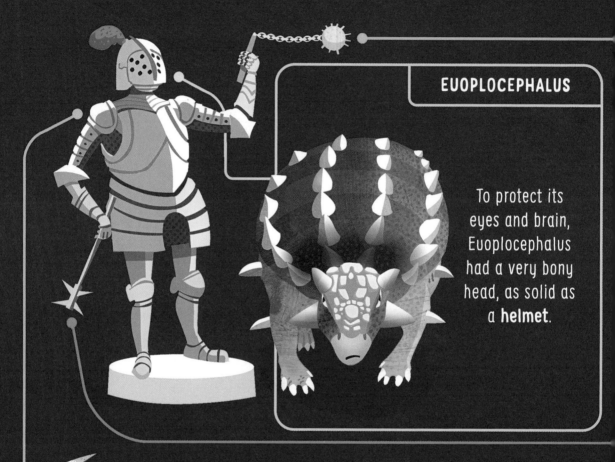

EUOPLOCEPHALUS

To protect its eyes and brain, Euoplocephalus had a very bony head, as solid as a **helmet**.

NODOSAURUS

The **plates** on a Nodosaurus's back were hard and chunky. No dinosaur could bite through them.

ANKYLOSAURUS

Ankylosaurus had a **club-shaped tail**. It was the perfect weapon for thwacking away attackers.

STEGOSAURUS

When a Stegosaurus swung its tail, the four sharp **spikes** at the end could deliver a painful blow.

SWOOSH

But what about those leaf shapes along its back?

They were too thin to stop dinosaurs from biting them, but they did make Stegosaurus look BIGGER and SCARIER.

The largest creatures ever to walk on Earth

Just one elephant can weigh as much as 60 people. But if you think that sounds heavy, you should take a look at these dinosaurs. They belong to a group of large dinosaurs called **sauropods**.

Even the very smallest sauropods were the same size as elephants.

WEIGHT OF SAUROPODS IN ELEPHANTS

1 ELEPHANT

SALTASAURUS

And the **biggest** sauropods, such as Argentinosaurus, could grow so heavy that they'd outweigh a whole herd of **twelve elephants** — or **720** people.

DIPLODOCUS — 3 ELEPHANTS

GIRAFFATITAN — 6 ELEPHANTS

DREADNOUGHTUS — 10 ELEPHANTS

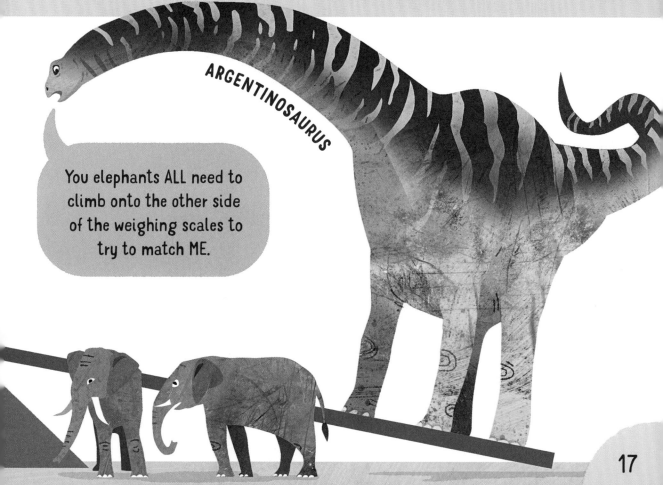

ARGENTINOSAURUS

You elephants ALL need to climb onto the other side of the weighing scales to try to match ME.

The island of Tyrannosaurus rex

Scientists guess that there were about
20,000 Tyrannosaurus rexes alive at a time.
But just one of these ferocious hunters was
enough to terrify other dinosaurs with its...

...amazing
eyesight

...thick, muscly tail

...bone-crunching
teeth

...springy feet

BEWARE
OF THE T. REXES!

...and razor-sharp claws.

Luckily for dinosaurs that lived elsewhere, every single
Tyrannosaurus rex was trapped on a huge island called
Laramidia, which is now part of the USA and Canada.

Tyrannosaurus Sue

There are only 30 or so **real** Tyrannosaurus rex skeletons in museums around the world. A few of these skeletons have nicknames inspired by the people who dug them up...

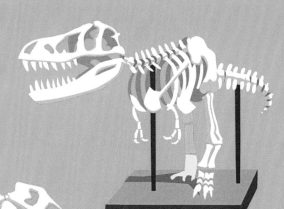

Stan
Stan Sacrison

Bucky
Bucky Derflinger

Sue
Sue Hendrickson

Who's Trix?

Trix

It's short for Beatrix. She used to be Queen of the Netherlands – and this skeleton is named after her.

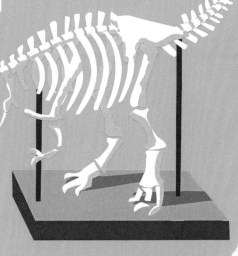

19

The secret sounds of dinosaurs

Did dinosaurs grunt, roar, hiss or squawk? The truth is that there's not much to know for certain about the **noises** they made.

But animals, such as alligators, can help scientists to imagine noisy dinosaurs...

GRRRRRRRR

Like many big animals, alligators make low sounds.

They rumble and grumble while keeping their jaws shut.

Maybe Allosaurus did the same... It was big, too, and alligators are relatives of dinosaurs.

GRRRR

RAH

Raaasss

Hang on... Dinosaurs on TV can be very noisy. WHO made these sounds?

If you ever hear a dinosaur on a computer game or TV show, you're actually listening to lots of different animals.

Crawww

oo ooo aaa aa

Harrgh

Heee-hawwww

sssssssss

Sound designers record their noises and blend them together to make up dinosaur sounds.

TRACK 2: SNARLING T. REX

21

From CHICKEN IMPERSONATOR to WRINKLE FACE

Whenever scientists discover a new type of dinosaur, they have the fun job of making up its **name**. To do this, they often join together words from languages, such as Latin, Ancient Greek and Mandarin Chinese.

Here you'll find the meanings hiding in all these dinosaurs' names...

GALLIMIMUS

CHICKEN IMPERSONATOR

COMPSOGNATHUS

DAINTY JAW

TYLOCEPHALE

LUMP HEAD

MEI

SLEEPY

BARYONYX

HEAVY CLAW

YINLONG

HIDDEN DRAGON

CARNOTAURUS

FLESH BULL

EUOPLOCEPHALUS

WELL-SHIELDED
HEAD

SINOCALLIOPTERYX

CHINESE
BEAUTIFUL FEATHER

What a pretty name!

WULONG

DANCING DRAGON

POLACANTHUS

MANY THORNS

APATOSAURUS

SNEAKY LIZARD

Scientists used to think Oviraptor stole eggs, but now they know it didn't.

OVIRAPTOR

EGG ROBBER

RUGOPS

WRINKLE FACE

In the footsteps of dinosaurs

When dinosaurs stomped across soft mud, they left behind **tracks**.

In hot weather, some muddy tracks dried hard, keeping their shapes.

It hasn't rained one drop since a BIG dinosaur trod here.

Oooooh!

Later, many layers of mud, as well as ash from volcanoes, piled up on top.

Then slowly, so very slowly, the mud underneath turned into **rock**.

And sometimes rocks, just like this one, are unearthed. So **real** dinosaur footprints can still be seen around the world.

A trip to the dinosaur dentist

Dentists sometimes take X-rays to examine their patients' **teeth**.
Here's what they'd find in these dinosaurs' mouths...

TYRANNOSAURUS REX

A Tyrannosaurus rex's longest tooth was as **big** as it is in this picture...

ACTUAL SIZE

BRACHIOSAURUS

Brachiosauruses had **gappy** teeth that were shaped like pegs. They were ideal for combing leaves off branches.

SAUROLOPHUS

The back of a Saurolophus's mouth was packed with little teeth in **stacks**. It used them to grind tough pine needles and twigs.

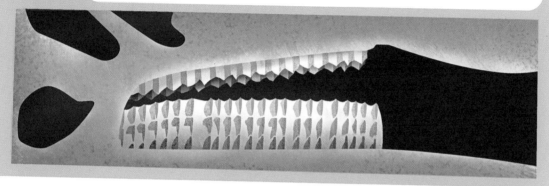

LIMUSAURUS

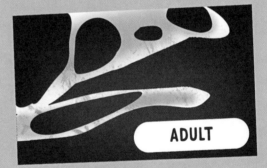

ADULT

YOUNG

What happened to this dinosaur's teeth?

It lost them as it grew up and stopped eating meat. Adult Limusauruses only needed toothless beaks to eat plants.

27

How ring-shaped nests kept dinosaur eggs safe

All mother dinosaurs laid eggs. They could be smaller than a golf ball or as big as a watermelon. What happened to the eggs before they hatched?

Just like birds, many dinosaurs **sat** on top of their eggs to keep them safe and warm.

CITIPATI

Heavyweight dinosaurs couldn't do this. They'd have crushed the shells!

EDMONTOSAURUS

To make their nests cosy, Edmontosauruses **lined** them with leaves.

SALTASAURUS

Some sauropods **buried** their eggs in hot parts of the ground. Then they left them behind.

But there were giant parents who found a **shatterproof** way to sit on their nests...

GIGANTORAPTOR

Gigantoraptor laid eggs in a ring and sat down in the middle without squashing them.

Oh yes! It's the same shape as my cake.

29

See inside dinosaur eggs

The shells of dinosaur **eggs** were either hard and crisp or soft and leathery. It took several weeks or even months for the babies inside them to grow.

When it was running out of room to get any bigger, this baby oviraptorosaur tucked its head between its legs.

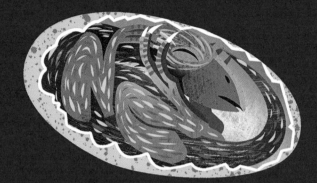

Inside this round egg, the baby curled up into a ball. It had a sharp point at the end of its snout.

It might have tapped the point against the shell to break its way out. Baby birds have something similar on their beaks.

Is it a unicorn?

No – it's a type of sauropod. Shh!

The baby teeth that NEVER chewed

When scientists took a very close look at the fossilized eggs of a dinosaur called **Massospondylus**, they discovered something **surprising**.

As a baby Massospondylus grew inside its egg...

...it formed not just one but **two** sets of tiny teeth in rows.

The baby lost one of the sets before it hatched.

Then it used the teeth that were left to chomp on plants.

Scientists are still trying to figure out what the lost teeth were for.

You'll never guess how the horns on a Triceratops changed

An adult Triceratops had one of the **largest** heads of any dinosaur.
To see how it grew, take a look at the pictures on this page.

As a baby, Triceratops had three little bumps for **horns** and a narrow **frill** above its neck.

Then its frill grew wider, and its horns grew bigger.

At first, the two horns above its eyes were straight.

Then they started to curve backwards...

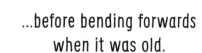

...before bending forwards when it was old.

The dinosaur with a trombone on its head

The head of a **Parasaurolophus** went through a series of extraordinary changes, too.

A young Parasaurolophus had a round lump on top of its head.

As it grew up, the lump began to stretch out...

...into a long **crest**, shaped like a banana.

HAARNK

Inside its crest, there were tubes that joined up with its nose.

Scientists guess they helped it to make honking sounds, just like a musician blowing through the tubes of a trombone.

I wish my nose could do that!

The planet of the dinosaurs

Dinosaurs couldn't read maps, of course, but none would recognize this picture of the world as its home. That's because the shapes of all the land and seas have **changed**.

Here's what the world looked like when different dinosaurs were alive...

EARTH NOW

70 MILLION YEARS AGO

90 MILLION YEARS AGO

PACHYCEPHALOSAURUS

That's more like it.

Much better!

SEGNOSAURUS

200 MILLION YEARS AGO

Why did the land move?

Here's my world.

LYCORHINUS

Because enormous pieces of rock under the ground and sea moved very, very slowly. They're still moving now.

Some parts of the world used to look and feel surprisingly **different**, too. Take Antarctica. Now it's the coldest place on Earth, where ice-loving penguins live.

But if penguins could travel back in time, they'd find dinosaurs living in warm forests on Antarctica instead.

Whoah – no snow!

WELCOME TO ANTARCTICA

120 MILLION YEARS AGO

IGUANODONTIDS

Why dinosaur poo ISN'T smelly

When is a rock not a rock? When it's a fossilized dinosaur **poo**! These types of fossils have lost their yucky smell, but they still contain some of the things that dinosaurs ate...

CRUNCHED BONES

ROTTEN WOOD

CRUSHED SNAIL SHELLS

Fossilized poos are called COPROLITES.

No smell at all!

In some coprolites, you can even see tunnels made by dung beetles. These insects eat poo when it's still soft.

Two of the **biggest** coprolites ever found are about the size of a basketball and a rolled-up yoga mat.

A wee mystery...

There's very little to know for certain about dinosaurs' **wee**. Any wee that they did do dried up in the sunshine or soaked into the ground, so it quickly vanished.

But there are a few strange fossils that look like this...

WATCH OUT!

And scientists think that the patterns in them were made when a dinosaur did a wee onto some sand.

The nose that knows

Rivers and river banks were far from safe when **Spinosaurus** was on the prowl. It had the **longest** body of all the meat eaters – and it was one of the only dinosaurs that could **swim**.

To paddle through the water, Spinosaurus waved its wide tail.

Like most animals, it couldn't smell a thing underwater, but its lengthy snout did help it to hunt.

What's this dinosaur searching for?

Fish to eat!

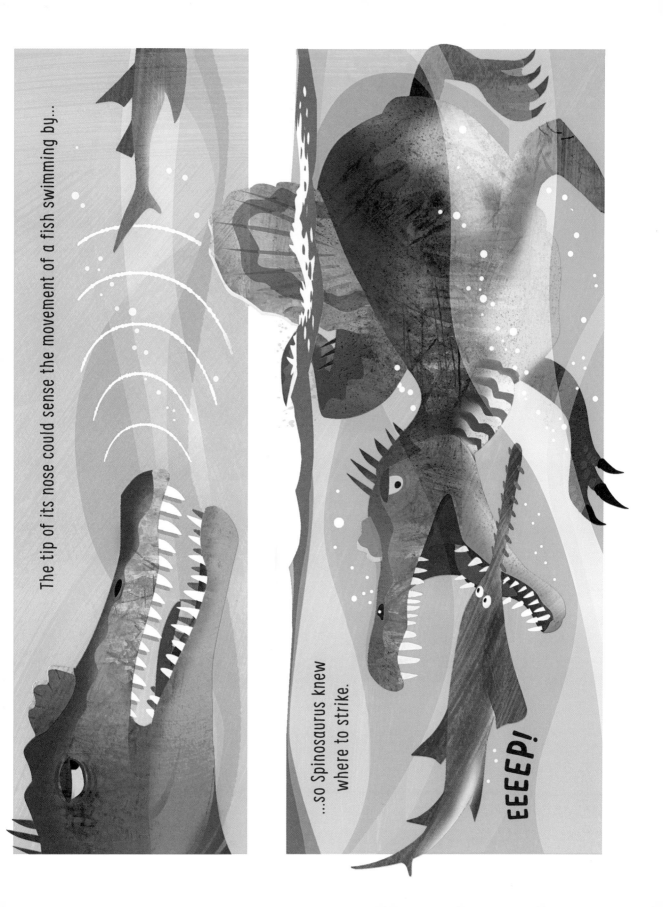

The tip of its nose could sense the movement of a fish swimming by...

...so Spinosaurus knew where to strike.

EEEEP!

What did dinosaurs get up to in the dark?

Take a look through these night vision binoculars to see who was wide **awake**...

My turn!

EDMONTOSAURUSES

These dinosaurs didn't know night from day. Their home near the top of the planet stayed dark all winter.

Other Edmontosauruses lived where it was very warm and sunny. Scientists think that they waited for darkness to search for food, so they didn't get too hot.

Its sharp hearing helped **Shuvuuia** to pinpoint insects scuttling beneath the desert sand.

Even in the pitch black of night, Shuvuuia knew exactly where to dig to find bugs to eat.

Why the first dinosaur experts had dinner inside an Iguanodon

Just 200 years ago, no one knew a single thing about dinosaurs.

People digging up dinosaur bones before then mistook them for the remains of...

...dragons

...enormous fish

...and **even** giants.

BUT IN 1842...

...British scientist Richard Owen made a huge discovery.

He worked out that three separate sets of fossils all came from the **same** group of animals. So he decided to call them **dinosaurs**.

I made up the name DINOSAUR. It means MIGHTY LIZARD in Ancient Greek.

TEN YEARS LATER...

...four life-size models of these dinosaurs went on display in London's Crystal Palace Park.

They didn't look exactly right, but they were the first ones ever seen.

These spikes actually belonged on the front feet.

TWO IGUANODONS

MEGALOSAURUS

HYLAEOSAURUS

A real Megalosaurus walked on two legs.

And the mould used to make one of the Iguanodons was the venue for a very special dinner...

...with Richard Owen and other dinosaur scientists as guests.

More soup?

Pigeon pie coming through...

The dinosaur models are still in Crystal Palace Park today.

Claws three times longer than bananas

Can you think what it would be like if your fingernails were to grow as long as a banana? And how about as long as three big bananas? Only then would you be a match for **Therizinosaurus**.

It had the LONGEST CLAWS of any animal ever.

Look at the size of them!

Therizinosaurus ate plants. It used its claws to hook dangling branches and pull them towards its mouth.

How Velociraptor kept its claws as sharp as needles

Velociraptor was about the size of a big dog. It had toothy jaws, a long tail, feathers all over its body and curved claws.

While hunting, Velociraptor could run quickly...

...with only two toes on each foot touching the ground.

It held its biggest claws up, so they never became blunt. They stayed perfectly pointy for pinning down little dinosaurs.

All tucked up?

Did dinosaurs sleep standing up? Did they lean against a tree? Or did they lie down? The way most dinosaurs slept is a mystery — but that's not the case for a little dinosaur called **Mei**.

THE SLEEPY DINOSAUR

Before drifting off to sleep, Mei nestled down on top of its legs.

It turned its head, and tucked it under one arm...

...and wrapped its tail around its body.

Two fossils show Mei fast asleep in this position.

While you sleep, your eyes often start to twitch.
This happens whenever you see things in your dreams.

Many animals' eyes do this in
their sleep, so it's possible that
sleeping dinosaurs' eyes twitched, too.

Maybe Mei dreamed
of hunting insects...

The creatures that lived on dinosaurs

If dinosaurs had looked very, very closely, they'd have spotted tiny insects clinging to their feathers.

Eww!

The insects had short antennae on their heads and strong mouthparts. They nibbled on dinosaur feathers for food.

Scientists know about these insects because they've found a few of them trapped inside pieces of **amber**. They're a type of fossil, too.

See the dots... Each one is an insect!

AMBER

But what's amber and how did they get in there?

48

The amber started out as a soft, sticky substance called **resin**.

It oozed out of broken tree trunks and branches.

If a feather fell off a dinosaur and landed on the resin, it got stuck. Then more resin covered the feather.

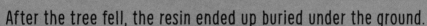

After the tree fell, the resin ended up buried under the ground.

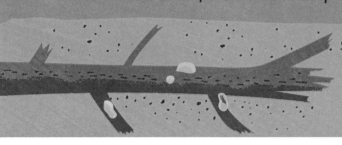

Over a very long time, and because of the weight of mud above, the resin turned hard and glassy, becoming amber.

Lots of things from dinosaur times have been spotted in amber, such as...

CRABS

ANTS

FLOWERS

MOSQUITOS

...as well as a baby dinosaur's tail.

Bite marks, bruises and wounds... OUCH

Stand back! **Fights** between dinosaurs could turn pretty ugly...

ZUUL **VS.** ZUUL

This dinosaur landed a mean blow with its tail.

It smashed the tips off its opponent's spikes.

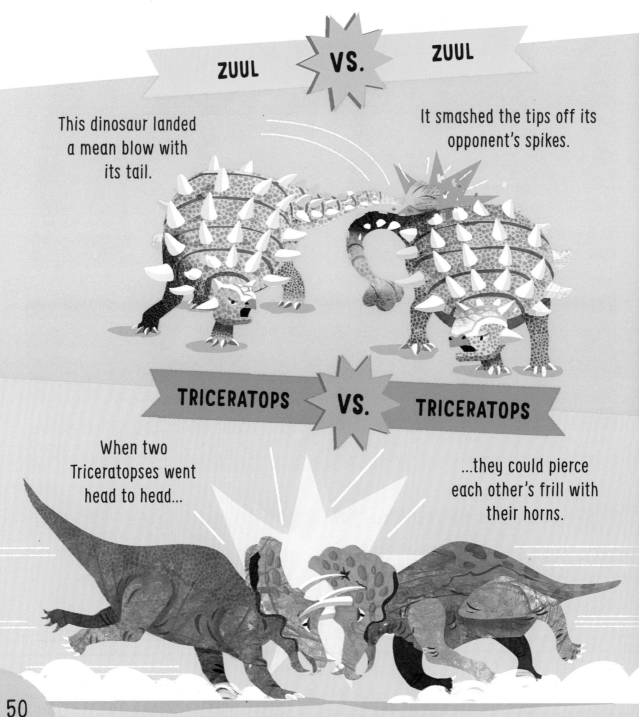

TRICERATOPS **VS.** TRICERATOPS

When two Triceratopses went head to head...

...they could pierce each other's frill with their horns.

DASPLETOSAURUS VS. DASPLETOSAURUS

Fighting Daspletosauruses locked jaws.

They kept on biting until one of them gave up.

All the injuries on these pages have been seen in fossils.

I feel a little scared...

51

Dinosaur-free skies...

Every kind of dinosaur lived on land. But if they ever looked up, they'd have seen **pterosaurs**, like these ones, flying in the air.

Little pterosaurs hunted insects.

ANUROGNATHUS

Bigger pterosaurs swooped down to catch fish or squid.

RHAMPHORHYNCHUS

...and dinosaur-free seas

Phew. Nothing scary here.

Not exactly... In dinosaur times, there were sharks, as well as creatures called plesiosaurs and mosasaurs that lived underwater.

SQAULICORAX

This type of shark no longer exists.

Pterosaurs didn't have scaly skin. They were covered in a fluffy fuzz that kept them warm.

The big crest on this male pterosaur's head probably helped to make it look impressive to female pterosaurs.

AFROTAPEJARA

PTERANODON

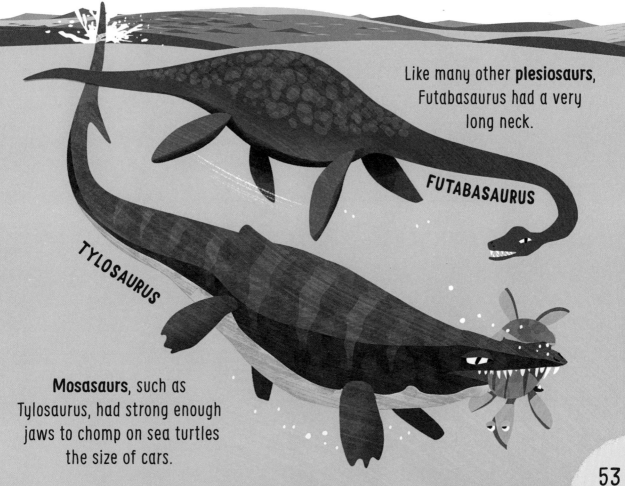

Like many other **plesiosaurs**, Futabasaurus had a very long neck.

FUTABASAURUS

TYLOSAURUS

Mosasaurs, such as Tylosaurus, had strong enough jaws to chomp on sea turtles the size of cars.

53

Dinosaur skull secrets

Amazing machines called CT scanners help doctors to see inside their patients' bodies. They can also reveal things about dinosaurs, such as what's inside their **skulls**...

Can you help me scan this SARMIENTOSAURUS skull next, please?

CT SCANNER

CT SCANNER IMAGE

When the skull goes into the scanner, a computer makes lots of pictures. Together, they reconstruct the shape and size of the **brain** from the hollow space that it used to fill.

ACROCANTHOSAURUS

BURIOLESTES

STEGOSAURUS

CT scans show that big dinosaurs didn't have particularly big brains.

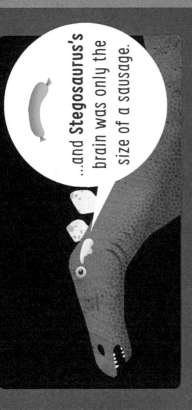

Sarmientosaurus's brain was smaller than an orange...

...and **Stegosaurus's** brain was only the size of a sausage.

There's a rounded part of the brain that works to detect smells.

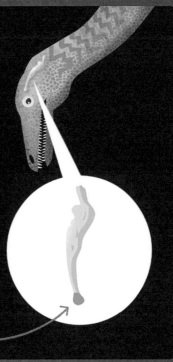

This part is much bigger in **Acrocanthosaurus...**

...so it probably had a much stronger sense of smell than **Buriolestes.**

Four heads are better than one

Life in the desert was tough for **Protoceratops** – especially when it was young.

Finding plants to eat in this dry, rocky landscape was a struggle. And there was always the looming threat of a bloodthirsty **Tarbosaurus**.

That's why young Protoceratopses joined forces in small groups.

They could search for food together and keep all their eyes peeled for danger.

Can we help? I think I saw some more leaves that way.

Underground hideaway

Oryctodromeus was hard to spot in its woodland home — unless you knew where to look...

Anyone there?

Oryctodromeus dug a **burrow** into the ground...

...where it and its babies could stay safe and warm.

Going out with a BANG

And then one day, 66 million years ago, **disaster** struck.

An **asteroid** – a giant space rock – hurtled towards Planet Earth.

It was even bigger than a mountain and landed with an almighty **CRASH**.

The dinosaurs didn't stand a chance.

Not quite the end...

The dinosaurs in these frames are part of a group called **theropods**. They're no longer around, of course, but every single **bird** in the world is a living theropod.

Yes, birds are the **one type of dinosaur** that's still around, flapping, pecking, hovering, squawking and chirping.

DEINONYCHUS

MACAW

CASSOWARY

They're all our LONG-LOST cousins on the wall.

FINCH

KINGFISHER

CURLEW

I bet you'll never look at birds in the same way again.

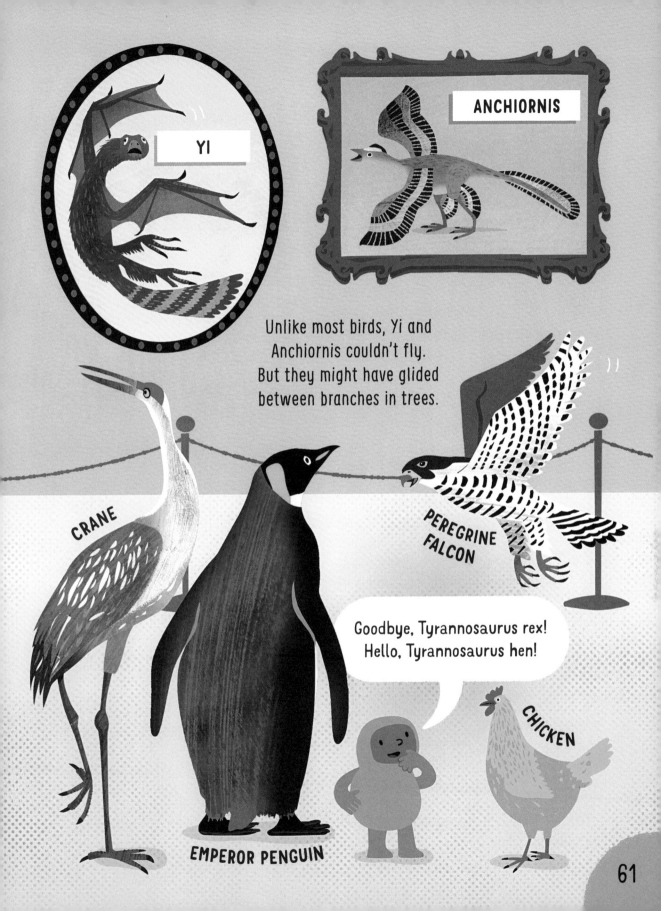

YI

ANCHIORNIS

Unlike most birds, Yi and Anchiornis couldn't fly. But they might have glided between branches in trees.

CRANE

PEREGRINE FALCON

Goodbye, Tyrannosaurus rex! Hello, Tyrannosaurus hen!

EMPEROR PENGUIN

CHICKEN

Glossary

Here you can find out what some of the words in this book **mean**...

amber – a yellow-brown **fossil** that used to be **resin**

Antarctica – the icy land and sea near the South Pole

antennae – feelers on the head of an insect

asteroid – a lump of rock in space

balance – the ability to stay upright without falling over

bristle – a stiff, threadlike spike

burrow – a hole or tunnel under the ground where some animals live

coprolite – a **fossilized** dinosaur poo

crest – a fleshy mound or feathery tuft on an animal's head

Cretaceous – the time when the last dinosaurs were around

fern – a plant with feathery leaves and no flowers

fossil – a rock-like thing left behind by ancient animals or plants

fossilized – turned into a **fossil**

frill – a bony or fleshy flap behind an animal's head

horn – a hard, pointed spike that grows from an animal's head

Jurassic – the time between the **Triassic** and the **Cretaceous**

mosasaur – an ancient sea creature with a wide tail

oviraptorosaur – a type of dinosaur that had feathers

plate – a thick, bony part on a dinosaur's body

plesiosaur – an ancient sea creature with a long or short neck

pterosaur – an ancient animal that could fly

resin – a sticky liquid made by some types of trees

sauropod – a type of big dinosaur

theropod – a type of dinosaur with hollow bones

track – a mark left behind by an animal when it moves

Triassic – the time when the first dinosaurs were around

twitch – to make small, jerky movements

Index

Series editor: Ruth Brocklehurst
Series designer: Helen Lee

First published in 2023 by Usborne Publishing Limited, 83-85 Saffron Hill, London EC1N 8RT, United Kingdom. usborne.com Copyright © 2023 Usborne Publishing Limited. The name Usborne and the Balloon logo are registered trade marks of Usborne Publishing Limited. All rights reserved. No part of this publication may be reproduced, stored in a retrieval system or transmitted in any form or by any means without prior permission of the publisher. UKE.

Usborne Publishing is not responsible and does not accept liability for the availability or content of any website other than its own, or for any exposure to harmful, offensive or inaccurate material which may appear on the Web. Usborne Publishing will have no liability for any damage or loss caused by viruses that may be downloaded as a result of browsing the sites it recommends.